My Book Series

Goals

"There are many ways to use these pages. You can draw, write, cut and paste pictures or articles. The most important part is that you contribute to your own series. Don't forget to write your name on the cover and fill out the author spot on the back. You can post your pages or get ideas on our Instagram @mybookserieson or visit our blog. "

Big goals can be over-whelming. They make you do things you never knew you could and test your nerves as your test your fears. Expressing your dreams through writing, drawing or other creating can help turn your dreams into goal and into reality.

I hope you fill this book with more ideas than it can contain.

Dream Big,
Christina

Who are you now?

What name do you go by? Age, hobbies, maybe a self-portrait.

What inspires you? Where do you most like to be? Why?

Goals

We all have many goals. Making a list shows you what directions to take, like a map. Fill these pages with goals. They can be simple or grand.

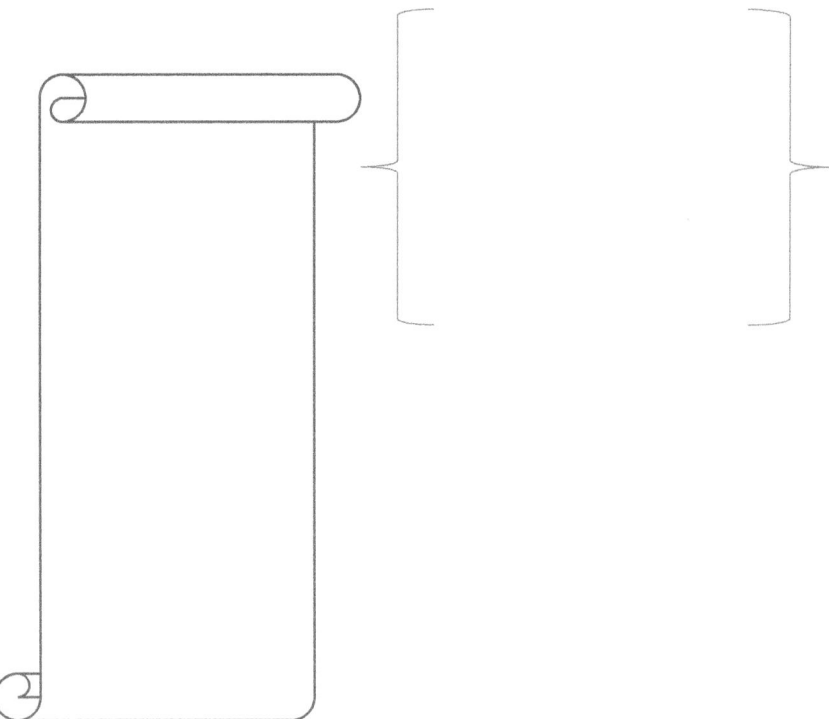

Health goals? Physical Goals?   Relationship. Work or career goals. Fun and recreation

Education goals? Creative goals? Spiritual. Financial. Travel. Living Space.

first five

Circle five you want the most and list below.

Be with Dreamers

5 people you've never met that you admire: 5 people you spend the most time with:

How do they share traits? How are they different?

Do you inspire each other to achieve goals? Even small ones? Or silly ones?

For the next page, *Vision*. Using newspapers, magazines or photos, cut and paste any images or phrases that having meaning to you. They should be true to what you want for the future.

Vision

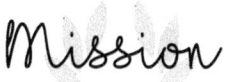

A statement should include an overall goal, purpose and focus for your life. Reflecting YOUR personality and a description of who you would like to become.

Who are you?

What do you want to do?

How do you want to do it?

Use the space above to try out some mission statements.
Ben and Jerry's statement "To make the best ice cream, in the nicest possible way"
Some people like to make a large vision board and place it where they can see it every day.
Mission statements can be placed on notes as a reminder.

People get overwhelmed by the idea of their goal. It is too big, too complicated. Where do you begin? Lists. You need to know and celebrate what you already have, what you are working on and what you want to develop your future.

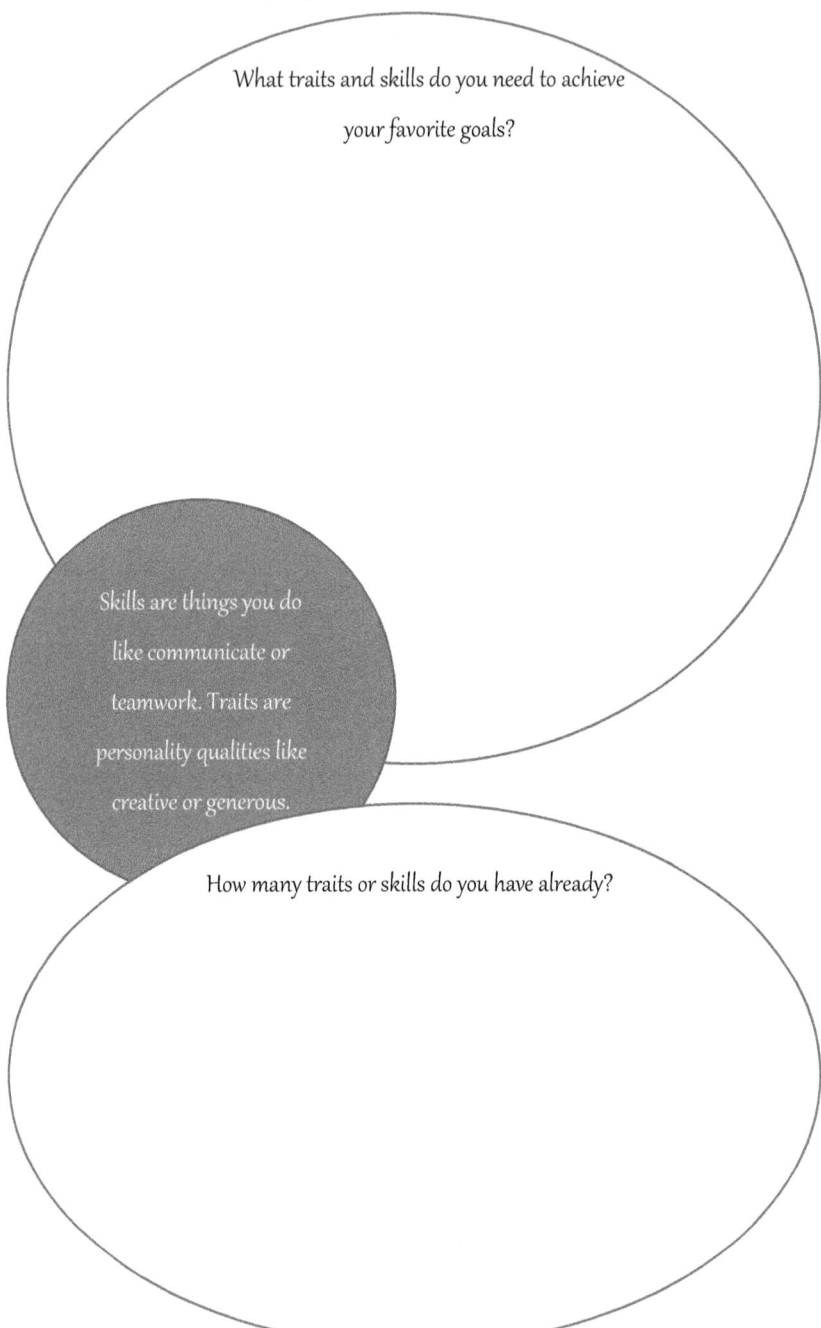

What traits and skills do you need to achieve your favorite goals?

Skills are things you do like communicate or teamwork. Traits are personality qualities like creative or generous.

How many traits or skills do you have already?

What are you working on now?

What do you need to work on?

Skills or traits to develop or habits to have.

The News

Date   First Edition

Reporter Wanted

Write your future success story, as if a journalist. What characteristics have helped you? What sets you apart from others? What do you really want to do and did you do it?

Don't forget to add a great headline and the date.

Disaster Preparation

Things may be difficult at times. Write, draw or collage a positive environment.

What does it look like? Who are your biggest fans?

Think about how that compares to your current environments.

Starting Planning

Take one of your goals and make it simplified by making a plan. List what you want to work on and the steps you need to complete it.

A goal is a dream with a deadline.

To Do

Short Term Goals — Start | Target | Completed Date

Long Term Goals — Start | Target | Completed Date

Gratitude

Being thankful is an important part to achieving your goals. Having a positive outlook can fuel you through the toughest times. Make a list of things you are grateful for.

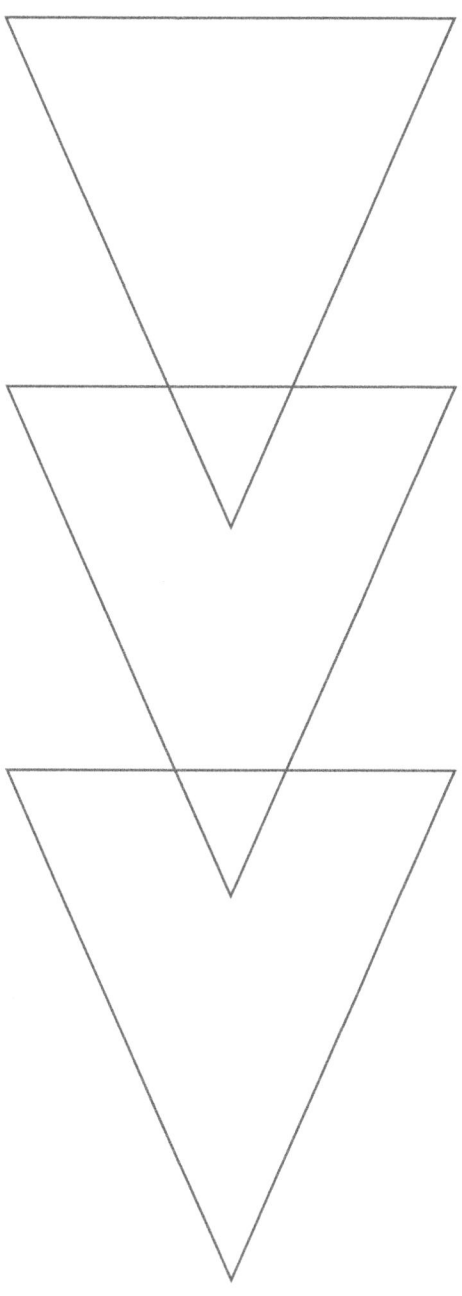

Favorite parts of your day ▽ Reasons to smile ▽ Something you love

Hindrances

What will you have to overcome? What can stand between you and your achievement?

What are some possible solutions?

Obstacles  Solutions

Don't let fear of what could happen make nothing happen.

What is the worst-case scenario? How would you handle it for the best outcome?

The quickest way to acquire
self-confidence is to do exactly what you
are afraid to do.

---

focus

It's easy to be distracted.

- △ Work on for set amount of time and reward yourself with free time.
- △ Make a list and work until you feel happy with what you accomplished.
- △ Complete one task at a time. Focus all your energy on one task. Often it takes less time if you work on one goal at a time.
- △ Remind yourself what your goals are. Look at your vision board and mission statement.
- △ Give yourself a small amount of time to declutter or organize the area around you.
- △ Play time, it's important to refresh your mind with something fun.
- △ Compare yourself to yourself. Are you better today than you were a year ago?
- △ Celebrate what's changed.
- △
- △
- △

The previous pages are about your dreams and plans. It will be good to read over what you've written as a reminder of where you want to go and how. Now, with all you have complied, it's time put your plan in to ACTION.

The next pages are samples for you to try. Find what works for you. What do you need to help keep you on track daily? Good luck!

Monday	Tuesday	Wednesday

Thursday	Friday	Saturday
		Sunday

Notes:

Monday

Tuesday

Wednesday

	M	T	W	R	F	S	S

Habit tracker

Expenses

This week's focus:

Thursday

Friday

Saturday

Sunday

Thankful

M	
T	
W	
R	
F	
S	
S	

Notes:

Next Week

Monday

Tuesday

Wednesday

Habit Tracker

Expenses

This week's focus:

	Thursday
	Friday
	Saturday
	Sunday

Thankful

M	
T	
W	
R	
F	
S	
S	

Notes:

Next Week

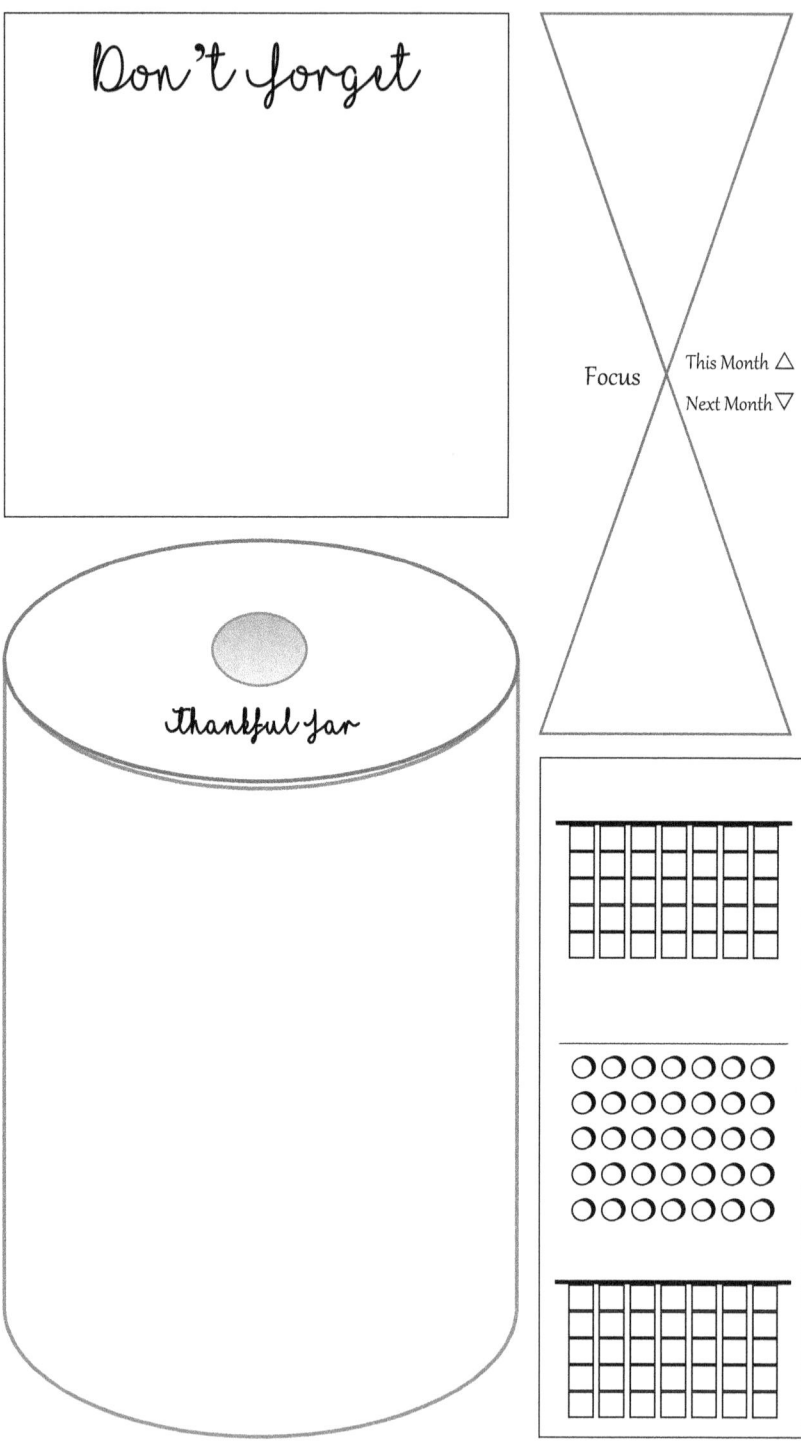

www.ingramcontent.com/pod-product-compliance
Lightning Source LLC
Chambersburg PA
CBHW051533240526
45471CB00019B/1322